dis ·

Mental Illness and its Affect
(influence)

Red Dashboard LLC Publishing

~

Z-composition Magazine
www.zombiepoetry.com

Cowboy Poetry Press.com

Annapurna Magazine.com

dis · or · der

Mental Illness and its Affect

(influence)

Volume III
Summer/2017

Red Dashboard LLC Publishing

ISBN- 13: 978-1539325123

Book cover artwork © 2017 Michael Baca
Book cover design © 2017 Red Dashboard LLC

Red Dashboard LLC co-Copy Editor/Proofreader-
Susan Spalt, Guest Anthology editor
Joshua Gray, Guest Anthology editor
Exzavia Willis, Junior poetry editor
Derrick Paulson, Senior fiction editor
Ian Austin, Junior fiction editor

Published by
Red Dashboard LLC Publishing
Princeton NJ 08540
www.reddashboard.com

/dis'ôrdər/
noun: disorder

1. a state of confusion.
"tiresome days of mess and disorder"
synonyms: untidiness, disorderliness, mess, disarray, chaos,
confusion, and more.

Mental disorder, also called a mental illness or psychiatric disorder
is a mental or behavioral pattern or anomaly that causes either
suffering or an impaired ability to function in ordinary life
(disability), and which is not developmentally or socially
normative. Mental disorders are generally defined by a
combination of how a person feels, acts, thinks, or perceives.

dis•or•der is dedicated to all of those (readers, poets, and writers who share their stories) who suffer from a mental illness and suffer with sufferers, fitting the range of disorders.

One in five adults experience mental illness problems every year—more than heart disease and cancer combined. Yet mental illness often goes undiagnosed and it is often not covered by insurance. Many people cannot afford treatment. The horror stories continue to be written: of adults strapped to stretchers in the halls of emergency rooms for days waiting for a bed, of children as young as ten separated from parents while they wait for treatment, of patients discharged without adequate follow-up or support, of police officers who injure or even kill those suffering with mental illness, of those lost to suicide. Yet in addition to the horror stories there are stories and poems of hope and healing. The poems in this book shine a light on the courage of those who are changing the face of mental illness by writing about it.

My heart goes out to those who love and are loved by people with these disorders. You are a brave world. These poems are a reflection of your strength. It is only when all of us speak of our experience with mental illness in ourselves, in our families, in those we love that the system will change.

NAMI website (National Alliance on Mental Illness)
NAMI Northern Virginia is the local, self-sustaining chapter of the National Alliance on Mental Illness, serving Alexandria, Arlington, Fairfax, Falls Church, and
Loudoun.
http://www.nami-northernvirginia.org/
Help Line: 703.968.4007

"Together on the Pathway to Wellness"

~ NAMI

Help Line: 703.968.4007

ACKNOWLEDGEMENTS

dis·or·der definition in
    Merriam-Webster Encyclopedia Britannica

"Only A Dream" First published in Carrboro Poetica, Old Mountain Press, 2012

"Aesthetics of Tissue Boxed Depression" originally published in The Bees Are Dead

"It's A Worry" first published in Anomalie, January 2015

"Motherly Love" first published in Yellow Chair Review, June 2016

"The Storm Before The Calm" from *True, False, None of the Above* (2016 Poiema Poetry Series); previously appeared in 2016 in True, False, None of the Above (Poiema Poetry Series).

"They Get In" (Entran, de todos modos) won first prize in the Aldaia Cuenta flash fiction contest 2015

"Oracular Ovaries" and "Hum Me Back to Life" will appear in In-Flight Literary Magazine, 2016-17

"Therapy" appeared in the January, 2017 issue of Anti-Heroin Chic.

"A Son is Born, the Second", appeared in It Must Be Heartbreaking, December, 2016

CONTENTS

POETRY

Poem On Anxiety Disorder 5
    Norbert Gora
Rainbows and Chameleons 6
    Brenda Ashby Berry
Only a Dream 7
Mother's Day 8
Breakdowns 9
    Susan Spalt
HAIKU #15 10
AKATHISIA 11
Side Effects 13
The Yakima Woman 16
OCD 17
    Tyson West
Oranges and Blues 18
Sparkling 19
    Erin Locks
Aesthetics of Tissue Boxed Depression 21
Oracular Ovaries 22
Hum Me Back to Life 25
Hieroglyphics in Slow Motion 26
    Nicole Melchionda
New Year's Eve, Cleveland 27
Alpha Centauri 28
Oubliette 29
Nest of Sorrow 30
    Rita Anderson
It's a Worry 31
Motherly Love 33
    Lynn White
The Storm Before the Calm 35
    Marjorie Maddox

Carousel 36

Internal Weather Patterns 37

       Nikki Anne Schmutz

Picking Scabs 39

Monday 41

The Gullet of Love 43

       John Berry

A Spider 45

Free 47

Untitled 48

       Robert A. Geise

At First, If You Don't Succeed 49

Depression, It Never Leaves You 50

A Song, An Old One 51

Namaste, and My Definition of Peace 52

       Elizabeth Akin Stelling

Almost Died Today 54

       Poppa Mac

The Elegy of Babel: A Poem for John 56

The Loony Bin Limericks 57

       Reynald Arthur Perry

A Son is Born, the Second 58

Therapy 59

       Elisabeth Horan

Hostess 61

Misplaced Burdens 62

       Rebecca Bonham

Hide The Guns 63

       Sylvia Freeman

The Calm Before 64

       MaryLisa DeDomenicis

The Battles 66

       Smokey Culver

Funny 68

       Iris N. Schwartz

Living With Depression 69

       Nichole Schroeder

FLASH FICTION

They Get In 77
        Anita Haas
Balloons 78
        Steve Young
Rear View Mirror 81
        Niles M. Reddick
Scramble 83
        Amelia Browning

NON-FICTION

Only Love Taps 91
        Nicole Melchionda
Dis-Order **99**
        Heather M. Browne

POETRY

Surrounded By Anxiety

Poem On Anxiety Disorder

by Norbert Gora

sky flows with fear
sidewalk bathed in uncertainty
streets full of terrifying people
it is the bread and butter of my life

suspicious glances
hurtful as a hunting knife
they open the gates
to the boundless universe of the paralyzing dread

alarms blaring in my mind
prompts to escape
closing the door to my heart
before the curious world

siren wail in my head
like condemned souls
generating panic
at maximum speed

I would like to
break the mirror of my anxiety
laugh at powdered glass
but a powerful demon
holds me captive in the grip of fright

Rainbows and Chameleons

by Brenda Ashby Berry

The boy, a precocious lad of many ages
trips through life with The Muse
as his only real companion.

A haphazard canvas of good intentions,
his swirling pastel manifestations,
muted vibrant dabblings,
exude the seesaw of multitudinous emotions
worn shamelessly upon his sleeve.

Twinkling melancholy eyes,
innocent sorrow filled grin –
peaceful façade of a tormented soul.
Cast forth from sleepy waters,
pitched about on riotous seas
with hallucinations his truest reality,
he combs imaginary shores for safe haven.
No tail long enough to steady a kite in the hurricane.
From the belfry, chapel bells resound silent prayers –
Return to the here and now.
A vulnerable heart guided to share a depth of meaning in shallow
words of a song yet to be sung.
There's untold wisdom in the nonsensical babbling's of The Fool
endlessly searching for rainbows in a cloudless sky
and chameleons on winter's dark night.

Only a Dream

by Susan Spalt

When you were a child you danced through my dreams.
I tucked you in every night and wished you sweet dreams.

I don't know when darkness began to fill the dreams.
When we began to lose you, we did not sleep, did not dream.

Some nights are good and you are in my dream
healthy and happy, singing in my dream.

Then you are gone. I am left with only a dream
turned stale, no one can preserve a dream.

The phone call is for you, it is not a dream.
I don't know where you are, Susan, except when I dream

Mother's Day

by Susan Spalt

Alone, her son spins circles of despair
builds a barbed wire prison
she cannot enter or understand.
His words attack like hornets.
When she cannot hide the stings
she looks at his picture,
the one of him as a baby,
and hopes that grief will stay hidden
In the corner as she waits
for the phone not to ring.

Breakdowns

by Susan Spalt

Sometimes I pick delicate lillies
and arrange them in a crystal vase,
write letters and sing quietly to my children.

But the storms always come back.
Thunderstorms with fierce lightening
devastating thunder, and tornadoes,
tornadoes that spin me off course,
suck the life out of me.

Senryu #273

by Tyson West

switch clicks
fingers fidgeting
keeps god alive

AKATHISIA

by Tyson West

Karen,
I confess the real reason
I want to return to my 77 Liberty singlewide
Its leaky windows and rattle trap doors failing gallantly hoping to stay
The toxic wind shifting over the Selkirks
To hang at the northwest corner of the Wishing Well Trailer Court
Is not because I don't want to see your sweet face.
I swear to God and Eli Lilly
Though sometimes I think they are one in the same
It is because of these side effects from the baby blue 4415 ovals
You check to see I haven't cheeked or hidden under my tongue.
Sure I'll bitch about the dry mouth and the pounds packed on carried
by my swollen feet
And the claim I lost all interest in my fantasy
Of undressing your smooth body
And holding your brown nipples against that angle of the full moon
Karen, I am so compliant here
Because I know I can't go
Unless you and Doc Gilpin wash me in the black blood of zyprexa
And say I can be released into the harmonics of not sharing popcorn
and the TV remote
For, Karen, you and Doc Gilpin and Eli Lilly all conspire to take me
away from me
And the ideas and inspirations that soar in shapes and colors you
cannot imagine
Cause the other God, the real God that talks to me
Graces me so I can see the Prince of Darkness
Because if I can't see his evil ass
I can't fight him and save us all
Especially when I am jerking in the gait of a monkey drunk
As if I live on rotted fruit alone
Please, Karen, let me go

Don't deprive the world or me from the glory of my destiny.
Had you been there at the Last Supper and made Jesus take his
thorzine
He might never have climbed to his moment of glory under the
golgothic sun
No less passionate than my spirit as I rise to defend
Your soft flesh, of course, and the entire world
Like a hero in a fresco on the ceiling of the Sistine Chapel.

SIDE EFFECTS

by Tyson West

Modern medicine masks serious side effects
Behind promises of nausea and projectile vomiting
Worse than a hope of sudden death or impotence lurks
The never disclosed side effect – gangrene of saintliness
The putrefied of countless dark haired teenagers
Whose meds dash their rote melodious OCD prayers
In romance languages with their easy rhymes
Now abilified into silence.
Irreparable harm flows not to mention starvation of the masochist
    spiritualists of neurotic Spanish girls veins flowing with Sufi
    blood
And the blue eyed Poles, let us not forget those mystic fillies who
    impale their virginity on the Black Madonna.
Birth control itself alters
The dusty poverty of a south Italian village where
The seventh daughter of Luigi and Sofia
Herself a seventh daughter will remain
In the soul pool never to become
Innocenzia - skinny and sickly - but curved enough that the whistling
    hyenas
Hanging at the Piazza della città
Hoot at her lame gazelle passing
No -- she is no breeder like big busted sister Gina
She stumbles on first whispers of the virgin at fourteen
Unsure in holymity it is not the mezzo soprano of some demoness
Or Satan singing counter tenor
Snaring for her soul
At sixteen the aura around statutes of Jesus glows with
More than a twist of estrogen in the blood.
St Cecelia weeps real tears
And gestures for Innocenzia's heart to follow

Luigi and Sofia
Counseling with Monsignor and Mother Superior
Seal her behind a convent's cloister where the course hands
Of Sisters Galla and Benedicta
Strip off her bodice and the soft cotton skirt that veils her cold thighs
But not enough to hid their sweetly sculpted outlines
Matronly sisters bleed her sorrows and mysteries
Then pleasure her in mortification of the flesh
They record her visions and scruples and miracles
Then comfort her when tuberculosis
Hollows out her lungs to leave a vacuum for
The breath of the Holy Ghost
Growing more beautiful the higher she climbs
She embraces delicious pain
That she offers up to the cross
To reach the clouds at twenty three
Then on the same page ten lines from the bottom should read:
Prozac to smooth out her scruples
Leaving cribbed cursive devotions recording her tortured ascent to
        make the pontiff weep.
Now doctors' orders and the hard little talismans
Rounds rectangles and ovals with runes of Lilly 4115, A-009 15 and
        SKF06 spell away the halos and auras
With her mention of visions and voices
Psychotropic potions like seraphim fly into her skull
Antibiotics cure the dread diseases
All kinds of Oxys whisper away the pain leaving
Nothing to offer to Jesus for his stint on the cross
Vitamins and supplements fatten her up
Prozac smooths out their scruples
Twelve step programs and group therapy abrate of the edges of
        neurosis
Birth control injections close out
Immaculate conceptions in a world with
No miracles

No beatification
No one to pray to intercede with Jesus
Just the devil's medicine with its side effects
The damnation of long painless life.

The Yakima Woman

by Tyson West

when
i
visit
the small ones
puddling around me
often my dead son will join us
karen, the pink rectangles you make me take may stop
loving legions of lucifer's exquisite torture
but soon my son cannot find me
small friends drift away
this old crone
alone
here
waits

.

OCD

by Tyson West

I must not tread upon the sidewalk crack
In fear of damage one lax step may do
And I will wash my filthy fingers too
Whenever I leave I always back track
To check the locks and light switch in my shack
Where broken plates, junk mail and rags accrue
I must not tread

Against all counseling my faith comes back
In spite of God's strength if I don't stand true
Upholding lines for salvation he drew
The devil will get his chance to attack
I must not tread

Oranges and Blues

by Erin Locks

living life without regrets
remorse
for the wicked is still
but a dream of blue
screaming skies cloudless
storms another day
young and wandering
orange horizons
 shining
  o'r the
deep blue
 sea
cease
 seize the day
orange and gray
fades to twilight
hey what
do we have
 left

Sparkling

by Erin Locks

wine
sparkling glow
　　i
should have known
　　better
　　my
　world
　seems
dark and yet
feels strangely
comforting
like a flood of
　memories
white and rose
colored glasses
　　filled
　　of us
　　you
　know now
　half full
sensations
　of the deep
purple reds and yellow whites
　　and
steely laughter
　　and
soft torture
　　in
　beds
　of flowers
　she glows
bees swarm

butterflies flutter
sun bright
  fantastic moons
    dreams
starry indigo skies
    we
do not change
   we are
Nothingness
life
is
everything
She said
spines tingly
mood numbing
wine
spills
into my
night
intrudes into
  my
 safety
sparkling
lingering
  into
the depths
 darkness

Aesthetics of Tissue Boxed Depression

by Nicole Melchionda

Tuxedoed in vanilla-crisped butterflies,
your exoskeleton makes illness
look pretty. If we paint
your asphyxiating phalanges right,
then no one sees disfiguring truth.

Hair, the dazzling output
of masked vestibular fusion,
perpetually threatens to collapse skulls
beneath practiced smiles.

The human face has natural
spigots that release pressure
to prevent anatomical
bombs, but we use
your corks of aloe-sodden cotton
to defuse leakage. Wintry boys
on television commercials
don't fool anyone.

Your fibers turn
cilia into razors.

Oracular Ovaries

by Nicole Melchionda

This morning I had a dream
that you were sixty-seven years
my senior, champion of my measly twenty
planetary revolutions.

It was Thanksgiving, my mother's best
friend's big family joined us.
Jess just wrote a book, unorthodox,
blending detective mystery and Greek mythology.
I sat next to her as Ryan sliced his thumb cutting the ham,
no turkeys to be found,
his blood spurts and screams a swatted gnat.
I bragged about your writing,
the novel you just finished in real life,
all three-hundred-twenty-plus pages.
You couldn't join us because you were still working
the job you have now, teaching Chinese children English.

Mother wanted to commemorate the day,
so, as usual, she herded us together
for a photo: Only anyone who cares
about Jess' new book can be in this picture.

You appeared, dressed in black,
with yawning forehead, stringy veins,
and same egg white smile.
I flew: out of my body joyfully, and toward your warmth
with love, I a starving moth, too infantile
and barbarous. I grabbed your hand
and dragged you into the mob.
Amidst the chaos you later fell asleep on the couch.
Cassie tried to wake you, lift you

as she made some cruel joke about God
to us, the outsiders, The Atheists.

I shoved her. I would be the one
to raise you, hold you. In the dream
I was not as surprised as I am now
by how overwhelming my need
to make love to your skeleton gripped me.
No years between us stifled feelings.
My stenciled grin combatted the rational fear
that you could die any minute, day, month—
Could you live a few more
years for me? I do not know how
to invisibly dissect a chest and decipher who is closest
to putrefaction. Life ceasing to exist,
yours, and empathetically mine,
wouldn't stop viciously circling us.

We sleep naked. This is the first dream I've had
where the panic leeches and won't shrivel
under my salty, depressive fluids.
My only consolation is to write this down
so I remember all the details for you.
You've confronted my morbidity,
and how I beg you to let me die first,
as if we could choose the moment
our DNA stops undressing and mating.
Soon you'll wake, head against trepidatious metronome,
mouth consoling areolic constellations,
hands smoothing stomped brow.
Everything will be okay again,
but I'll never forget our last words.

I was cleaning up the mess, packaging
leftovers and stowing them in the fridge.
Looking past your ashes, I sought to retrieve the ox.
I'm so glad you're here now.

Oh, you haven't eaten a thing.
Poor honey, let me fix you
a plate. You gently cusped my arm, tendons popping.
You told me that Mother was worried
about what will happen when you die.
My illness oozed subconsciously.
I mouthed the question from muscle memory.
You tried to hush the sobbing
with hearth-breast and murmurs.

I can't take a new breath
when it's been held too long anyway.

Hum Me Back to Life

by Nicole Melchionda

I watched you thread orchards
with fraying tongue
unaware I was Orion, metamorphically disfiguring.

Celestial clocks slipped down
the question marks of your ears,
posing, love at first silhouette.

Your spindly liver, my waxen stilts,
parabolic back against television sp(i)rits.

Hilt submerged- paralytic venom,
y(our) stunted evolution,
I-haven't-been-suicidal-in-five-years.

I know where your fury has gone:
broken doorknob, hitched-up skirts,
eggshells in the scramble.

Hieroglyphics in Slow Motion

by Nicole Melchionda

Aphasia twirls through skull-burst dreams
as the hippocampus quivers beneath depressive ice picks.
The biological landscape leaks vermilion
when self-unhinging crop circles
fossilize in skin.
This DNA unspirals between the blood
freckled pages it haunts.
Dust cannot be memorized
between each arterial design.

New Year's Eve, Cleveland

by Rita Anderson

Tradition is pork roast and sauerkraut,
for luck—an important predictor
the first meal of the new year.
Deep in the roaster on top of
the portable dishwasher a pork roast
sits smothered with onions, clove
stems scored in tac-tac fashion across its raw,
fatty back. Brown sugar bubbles melt
under the warm ginger ale she pours over.
Some spills in from her own drink, vodka
and an ice cube. She screams at her husband
for buying the wrong brand of canned cherries,
her voice traveling farther in this weather.
The argument has begun.
Searching for the heart of his silence,
she sends him back to the store.
The child wakes to a door slammed,
his boots crushing the thin ice beneath them;
winter's uncut grass cracks in its ice frame.
From the kitchen window, his wife watches him
drive away, then bangs pots around.
A twenty-eight pound turkey floats
in reddish water in the sink, salty hollow
exposed. Disappearing to refill her drink,
she lets the carrots run out of water,
burn on the stove.

Alpha Centauri

Sometimes I think of your body
when I'm on the elevator and I don't
care who sees, he whispers.

by Rita Anderson

I used to like the idea of our closest star
being eight years away. It made me feel
safe from invasion, or like the news could
finally put a lid on the planet's expansion craze.
In school, the distance was explained as such:
       If we took a picture of you today, *they* wouldn't
       see it until you were eight years older and
       had kids of your own. . .

I am not into kinky romanticism.
I don't dream of my misunderstood mother
singing an odd love song under the full blood moon
in a nightdress, which seems to be the *thing*
these days with the cappuccino set: To date
I've seen five movies and read four books
about people remembering, kindly, their mothers
as midnight snow dancers. I don't find depression
interesting because my mother was lonely.

When my son was weeks old and blue
from screaming himself into hiccups, I drove
around barefoot in pajamas, crying until I almost
ran out of gas. --Sometimes I want an audience,
but mostly I don't want witnesses
and I don't want words
to make pain beautiful.

Oubliette

[French for "the place of forgetting"]

by Rita Anderson

Mother, there is a sadness about you I am afraid
I've become. At twenty-two you worked around
a burnt thumb to scribble on a napkin to dad,
with his tuna-lunch, a surprise: *I wanted to tuck in
your favorite part, but my legs wouldn't cooperate.*

Where did you go until at thirty-four, you are at the fence
of the new house, feet lost in snow, the figure
unraveling? *To lose one's mother*, pouring another.

Warm nights, you flew in the station wagon across the field.
I pretended to sleep as my brothers rocked into me
the same way the spilled oranges rolled at your feet.

You'd wave the car door open, flashing the inside light.
It was a spaceship, you would tell me later, swearing
me to silence. *I was trying to communicate.* For years,
I worried they would take you away but you stayed to throw
me out--clothes on the lawn--when, at 19, I *knew so much.*

Now, I am older than you in my earliest memory, in pigtails
asking my dolls if they thought you looked old: *You are beautiful,*
I had sung, staying in my own bed to nightmare about
the endless climb to your room.

One thousand two hundred miles away now,
you call to wish me closer when to me
we have never been. I listen to your plans for "us "
to "share a place." *After I leave your father.*

29

Nest of Sorrow

by Rita Anderson

This time my father broke the phone, the plastic
cracking in the cradle, cord torn from the wall.

A mile away a train blew its warning: Clear the tracks.
My mother's voice shadowed him as he walked

through the house, preparing. He paused
in the girls' room, peering out the window

into the dark yard. Feigning sleep, I shivered
under my blanket, remembering the time a train

crashed, its cargo poisoning the air. But, we would
not evacuate tonight. . . *This is your damned family*,

my father seethed, pouring bleach into a large cup
and moving the bat to the front door while my mother

started a pot of coffee. Knowing it would be another
all-nighter, I said the rosary to keep a post with them

in spirit as we nested in our sorrow and never moved.

It's a Worry

by Lynn White

He bottled up his worries,
his fears,
and sealed them in
securely.
Put them inside a bottle firmly
corked.
Then he thought, suppose they grew

agitated
and, expanding with the heat
produced
forced the cork free from the bottle,
releasing all
those fears and anxieties to reoccupy
his being.

It was another worry
for him
to ponder and fret about.
He knew
a screw top bottle would have
been better,
would have kept them confined
more securely.

Too late
now though, to have that thought
done is done.
The best ideas are, always
too late.
Past has always passed.

And then,
another thought came to him,
so timely.

Maybe he could he transfer them,
move them
to the bottle with the screw
fastening
and screw them up tight
without
letting them out of the bottle.
Without
letting them escape.
Without
giving them
freedom,
freedom
to invade
his soul,
his dreams,
his being
his reason
for being.

Such a risk
though.
Such a worry.

First published in Anomalie, January 2015

Motherly Love

by Lynn White

I have spent a lifetime
trying to break away,
trying to break out,
trying to find myself.
Always on the edge,
always on the outside,
not quite a part,
of it, not quite
a beatnik,
or a mod,
hippy, or
punk.

I was early to realize that
what she wanted me to be
was what she had wanted
for herself, about her, not me.
I wanted to escape such love.
I thought I could escape.
I thought I had escaped.
And I did, surely I did
escape
some
of it.

But not all.
Not enough.
So even now I feel tethered.

After all this time of leaving
her behind,

I remain
unsure
of my
own.

The Storm Before the Calm

> "…the tempest in my mind
> Doth from my senses take all feeling else
> Save what beats there."
> -*King Lear*, William Shakespeare

by Marjorie Maddox

She doesn't know what rages, but each night
the pain, unpinned from logic, begins its slow spin
toward howl. Her words, flung in the vortex,
circle accusations, fly out at us,
stunned into silence while the tempest
in her brain keeps howling. Each night
she doesn't know what rages. We circle
her flailing body, try to unpin her pain
from the vortex that spins her howl.
Logic keeps silent. Night flies out at us,
accusing. It is a slow spin, this rage
that unpins her, flings her out into a vortex
she cannot name. Her brain's tempest
is the howl circling our nights. We flail
in silence, circling rage. Night unpins
our bodies. She doesn't know.
The tempest in her brain keeps howling
until rage unpins its pain
from vortex and out
flies silence.

Carousel

by Nikki Anne Schmutz

Today wasn't a day
to ride the carousel in my head.
No… it was more of a
dig-a-hole-and-crawl-in-it day -
when you mistake the sun
for an interrogation lamp,
and rummage for a gas mask to wear;
just in case the voices in your head are correct.

Even now, after the sun has set
I'm looking for reasons to hide -
the shadows may be conspiring again,
eager to sponge away the meager
amounts of liquid sunshine gathered
in the spirit of looking for misdirected goodness.
Maybe I'll ride my carousel tomorrow;
as long as I leave the shovel alone, and gas mask on.

Internal Weather Patterns

by Nikki Anne Schmutz

Despite the tempest inside
few words exit my mouth.

Thoughts tumble in a
never-ending mental
precipitative
fall
from mind to mouth where they gather -
trapped in perpetual cerebral fog.

There, they pool unable to form as sound
until they dissipate and are
expelled as breath -
lost to the world as silence
instead of words meant to be.

I regroup.

Straight-backed, I sit in the tempest
exacting a path of unspoken words.

Still I'm trapped in a tumble of
never-ending mental
precipitative
fall
from mind to mouth where they rattle
against each other in the fog.

They attempt to form legible sounds -
my tongue fights against my thoughts.

I stutter, I trip on sounds, I fumble isms.
I sigh defeat and laugh a white flag
into existence.

Few words dare to exit my mouth -
they provoke the tempest inside.

I purse my lips tightly
and allow my thoughts
        to trickle
                silently
internalizing as nothingness….

Picking Scabs

by John Berry

How will I know its enough—
this getting in touch with my feelings?

This picking of scabs I've grown
on my wounds; these gardens
grotesquely congealed,
blasted coagulant deserts blooming
prickly pear, saguaro spines—

airless Martian landscapes,
red rocky streams where bloody rivulets
trickled to a clotted crimson stop
on the back of my hand.

Deft index nail; just the right tool
for peeling this lid, this stony seal
over too few hugs,
this sarcophagus shroud draping
the child within.

When it lifts, whole or in pieces
and I've held it a while,
examined its colors,
bent it between finger and thumb,
tested its mettle with a delicate
toothy test
before casting it out—

will there be pink new skin
ready for raspberry thorns,
a feather's tickle,
the gentle caress of a lover's touch?

Or will beads of blood push
from this artesian flesh,
threaten to breach these jagged levies
barely containing
their pools of emotion?

Monday

(after the passing of David Bowie)

by John Berry

My coat on its hook
by the door of the workshop
injects its arm in the jamb.
It asks me not to leave.

Stay here, in the dust,
where its warm it says
with your smokes and your coffee
where we can play the music
left by the dead,
where we can listen
to poems
the laureates left
in their wake.

And there is, you know,
work to be done before you *die*
which could be any time,
if you don't mind me saying.

I do mind but leave all the same,
rubbing the last of the warmth
in my hands on my un-layered arms
and saying a prayer to patches of ice
that they will not be the ones
to break me.

Another door, inviting me in
saying nothing but *welcome,*
you've been gone forever

on the wiggling nubs and
kisses of yorkies.

Setting water to boil
and words to rest
uneasy, unfinished
on paper.

I nod to the Colonel
with his sack of ears,
cleaning his nails

the thin white Duke
with his shoes on the table,
looking over his shoulder
at the birds I am feeding.

The coffee steaming.
A fresh pack of cigarettes
in my pocket.
I pray once again to patches of ice
that they will be kind
when I'm laying there bleeding,

My coat on its hook by the door
smugly says
I knew you'd return—

the chuff and shush of the rasp
and the file muttering over a line
here or there
rounding the corners of stanzas.

The Gullet of Love

by John Berry

I know you are a poet
but what else do you do?
she asked, this woman
I knew from the chapel

and I divulged my secular life
in less than a sentence
as though I were brushing
some dust from my coat.

Carpentry, cabinets, you know
I said, dismissively nodding my head
to the shop

where it happens, where the noise
of whirling blades and bits,
the shush and the grumble of files
and rasps, the chatter of planes,
the talk of the nails

turns to the topic of food
and a cupboard housed in a room
beside other rooms wearing
mutual hats in the shape of a roof
and spectacle windows,
chairs, tables and beds
lazily chewing our bodies
to a comfortable paste
for a swallow which says
you are home.

Strange to think
of the being and doing
from here in this molar
of something like leather

my skin, my flesh, my seeds, my stem
the taste of the bitter and sweet
becoming as one
in the gullet of Love.

A Spider

by Robert A. Geise

In the dream,
you are a giant woolly tarantula
with its fangs impaling the skin
on the back of my neck.
It must be poison
because I am ill from the bite.
My will is not my own,
and for what seems like years,
I stumble through life
not feeling myself.

Then you're a tattoo on my arm,
a symmetrical black widow
dangling from its ink web
on my right biceps.
I carry you with me everywhere,
but you're largely out of sight,
and I do not speak of you
as often as I could
out of fear,
out of foolishness.

Suddenly,
you're a daddy longlegs,
bumbling across my torso,
tripping down my legs
and onto the ground.
You wander about the house,
appearing, disappearing,
reappearing,
silent in your tasks,

not needing nourishment,
not wanting another's touch.

Finally, you're a jumping spider,
calm and still,
unnervingly so.
You make no move to escape.
But when I look away for just a moment,
you've jumped for freedom.

Free

by Robert A. Geise

I find myself, since your departure, free
of happiness. I turn to anything
to change my world and live in ecstasy.

I take a yoga class, do some tai chi.
With all the time, I have to do something.
I find myself, since your departure, free.

I have no appetite, so I don't eat.
For six-pack abs, I'll starve entirely
to change my world and live in ecstasy.

Coke, marijuana, crystal meth and E...
To pay for heroin, I sell your ring.
Is anything, since your departure, free?

I fuck a bunch of guys with HIV
(who pound my ass raw hanging in a sling)
to change my world and live in ecstasy.

I can't remember if you left crying
or if I left you, as you lay dying.
I find myself, since your departure, free
to change my life and live in ecstasy.

Untitled

by Robert A. Geise

When I met you, I must have weighed a ton.
Clawing at my necktie, I'd glut my gut
with carbs and fat. But soon you were the one
who filled me up. Before long, my big butt
was not as big. My paunch seemed to deflate.
I started getting looks from other men.
It didn't seem to matter what I ate—
being with you was better than Fen-phen.
But then my pants began to droop; my hips
presented. My cheekbones made their debut.
Your interest waned, and our relationship
became dead weight. And I had not a clue.
I left the day it suddenly was clear:
Had you your way, I would just disappear.

At First, If You Don't Succeed

by Elizabeth Akin Stelling

Love yourself, simple as that.
It's something every girl should
hear early on. But not all of us
have father's to guide us in the ways
of love, mentally affecting us.
My Genie, stayed at the bottom
of his bottle. Hard to swallow,
right?

Daddy's on the floor again,
and my head hangs down.

After time, three marriages,
and a death of severe consequences,
I finally got a home run, of sorts.
You're looking for the ball park,
the new one they built just for you.
Banners outside say, "This is it!
You've arrived!"
Cheerleaders, bystanders, park employees, and everyone else, look
just like you. The score,
You 54, Them 54.

But the game is far from over.

Depression, It Never Leaves You

by Elizabeth Akin Stelling

When you're standing at a corner
where a glass door opens when a warm body comes near,
the cold, pressured
and molded sand,
unlike myself—from years of abuse.
it's hard to express, open up.
Maybe, a bit more today.

Cries are locked in that memory room.
Pain on the walls, dripping down,
coated snot green, with dirt and smells
only hospital rooms retain.
It bubbles up in the head,
waiting, to burst and blob
all in its path.

Ghost Busters never had anything on
this bigger than life monster at the end of that hall.
When you enter, the nurse is around the other side, dressed in white
clinging to another, sobbing.

I knew the lifeless body of the
fourteen year old female,
to whom I gave birth, Mommas heart—
stretched out on the gurney
would not sit up, smile
and throw her arms around me,
never again.

Mom's tears are drowning me, once again.

.

A Song, An Old One

"Shortnin' Bread" (also spelled "Shortenin' Bread," "Short'nin' Bread," or "Sho'tnin' Bread") is a song written by James Whitcomb Riley in 1900

by Elizabeth Akin Stelling

As Mom was baking, she would spout out a verse,
"Shortnin' shortnin', momma's little baby loves shortnin' bread."
And boy, *how she loved to bake*, and eat.
Joy soon became associated with eating, especially sweets
in my house, at my table.

Migrant boats over filled with slaves from the Ivory Coast,
spread so far, more than flour and shortnin'can.
Starvation made way for more to squeeze in,
like pushing more and more butter into the floury substance
laid out on the counter, under soft cool flour.

In my mind, dark red blood flowed down the wooden roller
as it had into the violent seas crossing over.
Our blood ran hot and fast, and with it 'mixed' black Indian.
Choctaw and Haitian. Field hands kneeded dough for the master's
meals, and what was left…scraps went to the children, mulatto and
white children.

With it came *crazy*. Came *mean*. The end of any old stick, it rose up—
to beat the subservient back into the disobedient child.

Put on the skillet, slip on the lid,
Mama's gonna make a little short'nin' bread.
That ain't all she's gonna do…

She's gonna cry all night and day, thinkin' of her own Momma.

Namaste, and My Definition of Peace

~ from the Urban Dictionary,
and a Found Poem of conscious thought.

by Elizabeth Akin Stelling

An ancient Sanskrit greeting still in everyday use in India and
especially on the trail in the Nepal Himalaya.

A father and mother remind their daughter,
You are contrite, overthink, but lovingly careful.

I first heard Namaste in my health food café,
July, 2009. In remembrance of my loss, Mom and Anelisa.

Translated roughly, it means "I bow to the God within you", or "The
Spirit within me salutes the Spirit in you" - a knowing that we are all
made from the same One Divine Consciousness.

Was I finally close to the corner of peace, within?
A street with no beginning and no ending;
light houses guiding, from inlet to inlet, across the world.

The more formal greeting Sanskrit Namascar pronounced NAH-
mah-scar is also used in India, though less frequently in Nepal.

And I repeat, daily. You have to,
with a smile, forced at times,
along with humor, to survive—
Depression is marshmallow peeps, covered in chocolate,
sweet with each bite.

It stems from the Hindi "Jai Bhagwan," and is also in common use,
and carries the same meaning.

nam·as·kar

ˌnäməsˈkär/ ;noun
a traditional Indian greeting or gesture of respect, made by bringing
the palms together before the face or chest and bowing.

I'm still searching. Always will.
One should never give up learning. Searching.
Filling the heart with positive beauty, that has whisked itself away;
in spite, a hole torn, and yearns
to pass by with no recourse.

I'm at the corner,
of First and Namaste,
will you join me?
The journey is always long,
But never lonely, when together,
hand in hand.

Almost Died Today

Poppa Mac
MSAR Service Dogs For Life

I almost died today
Wish I was surprised
Nothing special happened
Maybe then it'd be disguised

Started the day in pain
Like every day before
Woke up in my bed
Just knew what was in store

My mind's been busy
Thoughts are scattered
Nothing makes much sense
Like my life is shattered

Can't shake this feeling
Like I have no worth
Been a while since I smiled
Even question my birth

Hate how I feel now
But this is my life
I've caused way too much
Destruction and strife

Everyone would be better
If I wasn't around
Never even been born
Or six-feet in the ground

It's a hard way to live
Fighting to be in control
Getting mad at everything
Like living in a hole

Some call it depression
While others say suck up
I'm trying my hardest
That's when I met my pup

People think I rescued her
But she rescued me
For if we never met
Don't know where I'd be

Most likely would have died
Or in a hospital bed
Not caring for anything
Just wishing I was dead

My life will never be easy
I'm always gonna struggle
But now my dog senses
When I need a big snuggle

I know my day is coming
And my life will end
But it will not be today
Thanks to my furry friend

The Elegy of Babel: A Poem for John

> "We were wrong to call such things God, forgive us."
> —from "Symbolic Execution," by John E. Bongo

by Reynald Arthur Perry

Were the words we slurred
mere supple toys,
signal into noise,
the contusions of our tongues just rungs
of the ladder in the listless, listing tower,
jammed together from car parts,
false starts, broken hearts, errant farts
and physics?
Go with God.

Did the edifice of chaos crumble?
Did the proud stones crush our humble
skulls, toes and fingers?
How would, how could, how should
our rarefied minds have saved us?
Or, in their savage freedom,
did they softly enslave us?
Go with God.

The Loony Bin Limericks

by Reynald Arthur Perry

i.
So this is the price you feared paying
When you lost the game you were playing.
You ran out your string,
So savor this sting:
You were the beast you were slaying.

ii.
You come to a sad realization
That grief brings idealization.
If it's the truth that you fear,
They will welcome you here--
Give in to infantilization.

iii.
If there still is some truth you could study,
Years of lies have rendered it muddy
So use all your might
And burn ever so bright,
You'll only end up bruised and bloody.

iv.
Weigh anchor and then set your sail
For exciting new trials to fail.
Your dreams turned to dust,
You've none left to trust,
So just fall in love with betrayal.

A Son is Born, the Second

by Elisabeth Horan

My son cannot remember the day he came to
Lose his mother.

My son only knows I was sad before
And that now I'm feeling better.

I alone know the secret; the
date of the day he lost me -
And I'll tell you since I trust you:

It was the day my second was borne
Came out shrieking - ghouls after me, the sinner;
A lion roaring in the night -
A mauled honey badger.

Ah yes, he was lifted right out of the smiling incision
And laid skin to skin, on my breast.

And I remember thinking he looked odd, like a football player
Helmeted with hair -
Laying on the nurses table; red and writhing
A salamander underfoot.

And then I remember
My first-borne pointed at him and said... "out".

Therapy

by Elisabeth Horan

There is no free pass in this new born dawn
whether it be blue black or gold green
it's all hard work
it's all humbling.

This is the new me you see
the better one; the reinvented
the not so scary, beary one

The one that doesn't yell at the kids
the one that doesn't cry in the car
saying, why me, God, why?

This one's got pills
this one's got a friend that listens
so very patiently
every single goddamn week for
five - count 'em five whole years of
Wednesdays at one.

Where would you rather be -
chatting with Freud just for fun?

This new time's got a choke on me
tisn't easy being in the world now
as a member, not an inmate

My own warden.

My own crawl through a pipe of sewage
a Shawshank Redemption
the murderer was you old foe - so fuck you...
I'm Tim Robbins.

Hostess

By Rebecca Bonham

Do you enjoy that sense of calm when you walk into my home?

That is me, the energy I give, while absorbing all of yours.

You take from me without knowing. You give me your woes,
your fears, your anger.

I bear them on the narrow shoulders of my ego.

Devouring them, bite by evil bite, smiling in the process.

Pleasant conversation through the nauseated pain of carrying
your load.

Enjoy your calm, your peace, your serenity, for it costs me so.

Misplaced Burdens

by Rebecca Bonham

I lost my spark today.

I looked for it in the overturned garden of my soul.

I lifted the rocks and all that slithered out was despair.

I kneel and muddy my hands, trying to reconnect.

Then I see.

The frogs are bloated on pseudo-estrogen.

The gulls die as their bellies fill with plastic.

There I go, walking though the valley of my own destruction.

Watching only the ground.

Not seeing the world.

Hide the guns

by Sylvia Freeman

"He has a gun," she says, her phone voice calm.
I rush home,
the gun is lying on the floor beside the sofa
where he's snoring, his mouth open,
in exhausted sleep.
"He don't know what he's doing,"
"I've seen worse," the aide explains.
Once a calm and peaceful man,
he now erupts in rage,
lashing out at his dementia.
The only time he used a gun
was to show our children
how to shoot the mistletoe
from tops of Georgia trees .

Quick, before he wakes,
ransack drawers of shorts and socks
search through every pocket
large enough to hold destruction,
lift each corner of the mattress
look in closets, under beds,
find the bullets, all the weapons.

Throw away the knife
he said he'd use to scar my face,
so no one else would love me.
I take comfort from the aide,
her arm around my shoulder,
but I'm falling into darkness,
searching for a place to rest.

The Calm Before

-for a cutter

by MaryLisa DeDomenicis

Paralyzed,
and as though if
someone gut me
I could find relief,
spill some animal

scraping to claw
it's way out of me
out of me. Set it free –
drain and refill my blood
of what base creature

I have become
who guards herself
from you, and me,
and them, As if I could
rid myself of smidgens –

bits of pieces –
as if ridding myself
of myself
I could disappear –
yet still be here

as the ocean
when it hovers
in the sky above itself
halfway away
from the world

but still of the world.
A cycle, wounded.
I feel, heal, move.
I am still
in the world.

The Battles

~For a friend~

by Smokey Culver

You do not see it coming; there's no warning, it's just there
      Bi-polar hits you like a speeding train
The ones who know you wonder as they see your changes come
      your actions simply cannot be explained

The difference in one's personality from day to day
      it's time that people finally understand
This is not what you asked for, you just play the hand you're dealt
      you go through life and do the best you can

Today your generosity is out of your control
      tomorrow you are hoarding; what the hell?
There is no explanation for the changes you go through
      you feel yourself locked in your private cell

Then anger overtakes you, and it brings you to your knees
      behavior that you simply can't control
You know this is not you, but someone you don't recognize
      you're grasped within its unrelenting hold

They send you to a special place where treatment is assured
      a place where you will find "recovery"
But here you find yourself alone, imprisoned in these walls
      and you have given up your privacy

Sedated, you sit in a chair while staring, wondering
      you now see things through very different eyes
You gaze beyond the window looking at the outside world
      surroundings somehow you don't recognize

How can we judge you if we've never stepped into your shoes
      and known the battles you fight deep inside?
You never bargained for this; it's not where you want to be
      but there's no place to run, no place to hide

So, with these words, I hope you know I'm here for you, my friend
      and I will be here for you night and day
And as I look above, I say in all sincerity
      God, touch her with your healing hand, I pray...

Funny

by Iris N. Schwartz

At our local cinema I saw a comedy. I laughed.
Since last week I've read three police procedural novels.
Lapped them up like my cat slurps ricotta cheese.
And I want more.

This year I started giggling — actually emitted several "tee-hees."
I cowrote a play, attended a very witty one-man show.
Revised and performed my fiction and nonfiction.
Celebrated close to two years and two months with the man I love.

I'm a poet. Jewish. Misdiagnosed: *bipolar.*
Later diagnosed: *major depressive disorder.*
Congenital worrier. Yet I am focusing on light.
There must be something in the penal code about this.

I'll return to anger and darkness and poetry.
But I think I may have been irreparably damaged.
I feel like cracking a joke.

Living With Depression

by Nichole Schroeder

And I should have asked you to roll up your sleeves,
        drawn cartoons in black pen between the lines,
        stick figure superheroes in a blue and white wrist-world
            guarding red cargo
                from biting silver sharks.

And I should have cooked you quesadillas
        the nights you drifted home from therapy,
 cobwebs in your eyes like
            lacework, fading.

And I should have gone to your door
        on the nights when your tears added stars to the sky
        and sat outside
            and played old records
        gathered droplets from your cheeks and hung them as beads
          in strings from the ceiling as
fresh constellations—

you always loved stargazing—

and when you packed your boxes, your face
        more sky than sun,
            I should have slipped notes into all your old books,
        photographs into
your half-empty pill bottles,
tied soft ribbons around your therapy journals,
painted your fingernails
           neon candy lacquers.

I could have given you brightness.

I could have peeled apart your ribcage
        and sutured in fireflies
                dug the sun out from my tongue,
        and pressed it into your arteries, planted
                planets in your veins
                        to prevent future bleeding.

Now I stand
constellations ready in my hands
and offer them up
to the sky
        you left empty
Kinds of anxiety that I have:

Toddler anxiety,
the kind of anxiety that follows you around and clings to the back of
your knees
that makes faces behind your back
that bangs spoons on pots and pans,
throws tantrums in the supermarket when you won't buy it's favorite
cereal—
anxiety that pouts when I ignore it
and gets indulged more than it should.

Cancer anxiety, fear of something growing in an unseen place.

Pregnancy anxiety,
the anxiety of immaculate conception,
anxiety that god himself gifted unto me, tore
 a rib out of Sylvia Plath and planted it, *this will be your burden:*
may you always be insecure and have men talk over you.

Man anxiety,
man-looking-at-me-talking-to-me-what-if-he-likes-me-what-if-he-
wants-to-get-married-and-have-a-million-babies-what-if-he's-
uncircumsized-what-if-I-find-that-out-the-hard-way-what-if-in-his-

faith-they-don't-use-condoms-what-if-the-condom-breaks-back-to-
the-last-point-anxiety,
what-if –he-likes-me-but-in-more-of-a-follow-you-home-and-write-
you-into-fanfiction-about-himself-kinda-way anxiety,
oh god he's looking anxiety—
anxiety of being looked at, of not being looked at enough.

Lover anxiety,
the kind that snores and pulls off all the covers and elbows you late at
night,
runs off before you wake up the next morning
leaving the bed empty and cold.

Anxiety that my pets will die.
Anxiety that I will die and my pets will never understand what
happened to me.

Void anxiety,
a voice in my head that tells me to look away
whenever I see dark rooms or corners or shadows
because they might see me back—
anxiety that tells me to look away when I see people I love
because they may see me back.
Anxiety that is shy and nagging.

Parent anxiety
empty nesting,
too attached to let me go.

The world breaks everyone,
and afterward,
some are strong at the broken places.

—Ernest Hemingway

FLASH FICTION

They Get In

by Anita Haas

I tiptoe to my apartment door. I open the three locks. Yes, three, but it still isn't enough. They get in anyway.

Through the window, from the roof, whatever. They get in.

I put down my shopping bags. I used to worry that I would walk in on them, but now I know they have spies to warn them I'm coming. So I'm not worried.

Not too much.

I go to the kitchen and open the fridge. They've been here. It's obvious. A carrot is leaning against a juice carton. In the vegetable drawer a chicken leg I had put in the freezer peaks out from between some lettuce leaves. It is thawed out now. Thank God I found it, or it would go bad. What a waste!

I sigh, take off my jacket and shoes, but I can't find my slippers. At last I locate them in the bathtub.

My toothbrush is in the cutlery drawer.

When I tell people these things, they think I am crazy. I see it in their eyes. I don't blame them. I would think so too.

But I know it's really happening.

Just don't know why.

Balloons

by Steve Young

By seven-thirty, a posse of kids had cut loose the helium
balloons. They floated up to the high ceilings and hung belly to belly,
their tethers dangling just out of reach. One rubbed up against the
stove pipe and exploded with a horrendous bang, eliciting shrieks of
laughter from the kids and startled smiles from the adults. So far, the
children were the life of Raymond's thirty-fifth birthday party, the
only ones who seemed to want to be there at all.
Ironically, when Janet had suggested that children be invited, too,
Raymond had shook his head and howled: "No, no, no!"

"It's a Sunday night," Janet said, her arms crossed, her voice
low and slightly brittle. "We can't ask all of them to get sitters."

"I don't want any of this. It's too much. Just cancel the whole
thing!" He buried his head in his arms.

She placed a hand on his shoulder. Her voice softened.
"Emily and Jordan will keep them entertained. Don't worry. It'll be
okay, it really will."

It turned out the children were easier for Raymond to deal
with than the adults, anyway, who stayed huddled in the kitchen and
living room in uncomfortable clots, as if they feared more explosions.
When Raymond entered one of these rooms, they greeted him with
exaggerated, beaming smiles, smiles he was sure turned to frowns of
disapproval the minute he turned his back. The party was Janet's idea,
and these were all Janet's friends. Raymond had no friends anymore.
Somehow, over the past year, they had all dropped off the edge of
the earth.

Soon the posse roped Raymond into playing hide and seek.
The kids scattered through the house like jubilant thieves. The old
post-and-beam was fun to hide in because of its odd, dark corners.
But Raymond hid in the bathroom, small and stuffed with the
accoutrements of four souls living in the same cramped space, he and
Janet and Jordan and Emily. It was located at the end of the hall from

the kitchen, beside the spare room, where he mostly slept nights alone now.

He shut off the light, stepped into the tub and stood behind the half-drawn shower curtain. The perfect hiding place. Too perfect; the kids apparently gave up and forgot about him. From somewhere distant, through the party noise, he could make out the trills of Jordan and Emily's excited laughter, the thumping of kids' feet on the stairs. But he lingered, stood rooted in the darkness, cherishing this thin and precarious sanctuary, the innocent smells of Ivory soap, Janet's apricot hair conditioner. A strange, whimsical feeling overcame him, hiding so successfully in his own home, in the middle of his own birthday party. At the center of things, yet invisible.

The light went on and two women entered talking, closed the door after them. He froze behind the curtain, held his breath, not daring to exhale. He recognized their voices, two of Janet's volunteers down at the Newbury library, Mrs. Bliss and Mrs. Foreman, middle-aged, one with hennaed hair, the other gone over to gray, with first names long forgotten by him. A musty scent of perfume tickled past his nose. They were doing some fussing near the sink, he couldn't quite make out what it was.

"See? I have to go in every week just to have the roots done. Or do it myself." Mrs. Bliss's despairing voice came to him shockingly intimate.

"It's not so bad. You can hardly see any gray," Mrs. Foreman said. Her voice was scratchy and slightly irritable.

"Carol thinks I should try another kind of rinse next time. She says it lasts longer and I won't have to bother so much."

"I still like the henna. It goes with your eyes. Oh God, look at this! This piece just won't stay. That's why I'm thinking of getting another perm."

"You don't need another perm. It looks lovely as it is."

"The whole thing sort of sags."

"Nonsense. You just need to pin that one piece up. You have a bobby pin on you?"

"No, no, of course not. I always forget."

"I don't either. Maybe Janet does. Let's look in here." The medicine cabinet squealed open.

One of the women gave a low whistle, the other groaned.

"No wonder he always looks so zombied out," Mrs. Bliss said at last.

"That's why he lost his job, you know. It wasn't the economy, like she said." Mrs. Foreman's voice was low and furtive, but perfectly clear. "Carol told me he tried to bash his brains in with a hammer during one of his so-called panic attacks. She saw the welts. Then he poured gasoline over himself and would've set himself on fire if poor Janet hadn't stopped him. The man's a loon, he's plumb out of control."

"I guess all these pills are to calm him down."

"They probably make him more crazy. Poor Janet and those poor children, is all I have to say." The medicine cabinet swung shut. "Well, no bobby pins in there. You'll have to stick it behind your ear, I guess."

The door opened, the light was extinguished. Laughter, dance music, giddy chatter spilled into the bathroom again but he stayed paralyzed behind the curtain. He felt as if he might finally dissolve. He felt as weightless as the helium balloons bumping gently against the ceilings, searching for an opening to the sky. A pink, a violet, a blue one -- the colors of his pills. If it weren't for the ballast, the tether of years, of memory, of obligation, he could float off forever, too. Maybe he still could if he tried: free, alone, a hollow mote ascending, disappearing into the heavens.

Rear View Mirror

By Niles M. Reddick

After a short visit when my mother-in-law drove drunk through the neighborhood with my two-year-old daughter sitting in the backseat, no car seat, no seat belt, I was done. I told my wife who was just as appalled and angry as me: "She can kill herself for all I care, but she's not taking our daughter out with her."

A pathological liar, alcoholic, prescription drug addict who abandoned her children with their father after a romp with the local butcher, Fran had been married eight times that we were actually aware of, though she only confessed four. Each conversation on her visits ended before sun down because she was tired. She'd close the door to the spare bedroom and make multiple trips to the refrigerator to refill her 7-11 plastic mug with one-fourth Lemonade, Sprite, or whatever was available, and three-fourths vodka (I had faked need for a Tums and watched her out of the corner of my eyes).

Years of abuse had taken toll. She had gone from slim and high energy, tanned and hair consistently dyed to bloated, slow and unkempt, at one time with a skunk hair look, partly black and partly white. The more she drank, the more she droned on about how she'd been wronged in her first marriage, how hard she'd work to support her four children, how hard she'd worked as a nurse her entire career, how she attended church, and how she believed in Jesus. Most times, my wife left the room to check on children and never returned, me sitting and watching television and trying to avoid, an occasional uh-huh coming out just to play nice. I knew the only times she went to church was when she passed out in front of the television and woke up to a sermon, and I had heard how she'd supported her children, using them to manipulate their father into money for needs that she ended up spending on herself.

In all her conversations, she never admitted to bad choices, didn't admit she had any sort of problems with alcohol or drugs, and refused to accept that she'd abandoned her children, citing her trips at holidays with gifts galore as if store-bought plastic toys made up for rejection by a mother. She never admitted she was on the phone when her second daughter nearly drowned in the tub and suffered permanent hearing loss or that she was carrying on in her dramatic fashion when one of her sons took an overdose of an aunt's medication that had been left on the counter because he thought the pills were candy.

Now, "retired" because she has no license to work as a nurse, she sucks in nicotine all day on the back porch of her other daughter's condo where she lives rent free. I'm convinced if her daughter could hear, Fran would be homeless. Her Social Security check ought to be enough with no monthly bills, particularly when Medicare and Medicaid should cover her health issues, some of which are mysterious back pain that multiple physicians prescribe addictive pain killers because she convinces them in their own language it's the only thing that helps. She obeys the rule of waiting until after lunch to down the vodka because she believes drinking it before lunch would indicate a problem. She makes calls to each of her children, her siblings, and a handful of others, and lies and pits them against each other, except that they understand. She tries to get them to send money to help with medical expenses, and she plays the tragic role of the victim, of one who is entitled, never quite seeing an accurate reflection of her life in the rear view mirror.

Scramble

By Amelia Browning

The first time Mom talked to me about killing herself, she was cooking something called "spinach scramble."

Curled up in my beanbag chair, totally absorbed in a "Magic Tree House" book, I slowly became aware that Mom was sobbing in the kitchen. Reluctantly, I left my bedroom to see what was going on and made my way through the tiny trail between the towering piles of clutter in the dim hallway. I stubbed my toe on a hardback book buried beneath twenty dirty towels that had languished there for months, then shifted aside a stack of empty wicker baskets that no one was allowed to throw out. I made a mental note to ask Dad (actually my step-dad) to replace the light bulb in the hallway when he got home from work. I didn't blame him for his long hours. I wished I had to go to work sometimes, too, so I could get away from this place.

She was sauteing things in a pan- spinach, ground hamburger, mushrooms- and crying heavily. When I walked in and quietly said, "Hi, Mom," she took the pan off the burner, shut the stove off, and said, "Ellie, come here. I want to talk to you but I need to keep an eye on Sophie." I followed her into the living room and sat on the floor. Various crumbs and lint clung to my clothes from the carpet that hadn't been vacuumed since before baby Ian came home from the hospital. Mom sat on the small spot on the striped couch that wasn't covered in junk. Cotton stuffing poured out of the cushions in several places, a slow soft destruction that no one had the energy to mend- if they even noticed it.

"Everything is just really, really hard, Ellie," she sobbed openly, letting her face get red and blotchy, tears and snot all over her cheeks and chin. She reached out and squeezed my cold hand in her dry, warm one. "It's just really hard."

"It would be nice to just be done and go and see Heavenly Father, wouldn't it?" she asked. I didn't want to say yes. This conversation already felt dangerous.

"I don't know," I replied.

She cried more and I didn't say a word. I should have said, "I'm sorry you're sad, Mommy. I love you." I *did* love her and I *was* sorry she was sad. But those words didn't come to me, because I also felt a sudden astonishment that knocked me silent. Gripped by a sense of inadequacy so deep I've yet to shake it, I sat and listened to her. That was all I could do.

"The Celestial Kingdom is the most beautiful place you can imagine. It's filled with trees and flowers more beautiful than anything on earth. No one hurts there or has any problems. But you know that from Sunday school, don't you? In Heaven you just feel joy and love and a really peaceful feeling, all the time," she wept. I knew what she was talking about and I felt extremely anxious. She wanted me to agree with her. And she needed to wipe her nose, but I didn't know where to begin to look for a box of tissues in all the mess. I wanted Dad to come home and comfort her. I knew I could expect him after dinner, but before we went to bed. He always made that a point, to be home to tell us goodnight.

"You know Daddy loves us so much. He loves me, and you, and Sophie, and Ian. I'm not sad because of him, okay?"

"Okay, Mom."

"I've just been thinking about how hard it is in this life, and I can't stand the thought of any of my babies growing up to live through all of the hard things I've had to live through. It breaks my heart to even think for one second about any of my babies suffering. I can't stand it!"

Six-month-old Ian wailed from the other room. She got up, checked on him, came back. Sophie played with her toys on the living room floor, dwarfed by the heaps of clothes, boxes of books, and stacks of junk mail surrounding her. All the curtains and blinds were shut so that neighbors who might stop by couldn't see inside the house. In the dim light, Soph's white-blond hair glowed like an angel's. She babbled happily, and Mom smiled through her tear-stained face. "My babies..."

"I'm not a baby, Mom. I'm *seven*," I reminded her.

"I know, honey," she squeezed my hand again. "But you're still young enough that if you died, you would go straight to the Celestial Kingdom. Do you know that? Because Heavenly Father and Jesus know that all children are innocent. This is what I'm trying to tell you... if you, and me, and Sophie and Ian went for a pretty drive, and we just... drove off into a beautiful blue lake... if something like that happened? You would go straight to the most beautiful, peaceful place. You would never have to go through life and deal with things like I've had to. You'd just be instantly happy, for eternity. It would be a gift, if that happened..."

Her voice catching on the words, she continued, "I could do that for you, for my babies. We could just stop all this horribleness and go together."

"I don't want to," I said.

Or maybe I said, "Mom, when's Dad coming home?"

Or possibly it was, "Can we eat dinner now? I'm hungry." I don't know. I don't remember what I said, or what she said next.

Dad came home, later, looking wild-eyed and terrified, I think. But maybe my memory filled that in incorrectly: maybe he never knew. I don't remember the rest of the evening with any clarity.

It never occurred to me to tell Dad about any of Mom's ideas she shared with me when she was sad. It wasn't something I debated in my mind; I mean it just literally did not occur to me because by this time, silence was my default. I didn't go to him or Mom with stories of my biological dad being mean and drunk on my weekends with him. I didn't ask them for help with school projects I was overwhelmed with, choosing to just not do them and then fake sick and stay home on the due date. I didn't say anything about the angry criticisms of our junk-filled house and unkempt yard, relayed to me through the kids of the other homeowners in the neighborhood. It was so clear that Mom and Dad had enough problems to deal with- I couldn't bear to burden either of them with anything else.

But in the months that followed that talk with Mom, whenever she was driving my little half-sister, half-brother, and I in the car, I worried that maybe she was sad again. Always on edge when we drove beside a river or large body of water, I worried that something might happen, and what would I do or feel if it did?

Sometimes postpartum depression ends in tragedy and lurid headlines, but we never once drove off into any lakes, nor do I think it was a true, real danger. Mom's pain cropped up in the form of crying spells and suicidal plans multiple times over the years, especially after she started taking Ambien every night and then staying up to talk instead of going to sleep, the next day not remembering all the things she'd said that I couldn't bear to hear.

In the conservative, religious culture we were a part of, there's enormous pressure for a woman to be seen as a good "homemaker," and a severe stigma when certain standards aren't met. Her refusal to throw anything away or let anyone help her clean her chaotic nightmare of a house was more than enough to get people talking about her behind her back. Why would she share her struggles with depression with a bunch of sunny-faced, bread-baking neighbors who would do more harm than good with their gossip and judgment? I can't imagine how alone Mom must have felt, especially as an only child with few living relatives.

She had three young, needy children; no support in fighting her depression and anxiety; nothing but her church to comfort her existential dread- and despite what she claims about the peace her beliefs bring her, I know she suffered so much, and still does, and I feel sorry for her.

She was 31 with three kids who she wanted to leave "this life" with. I'm not so ignorant as to think I'd do any better, with her background and in her situation. I understand it, to the extent that I can right now.

I never once doubted she loved us. That was crystal clear to me. If she hadn't loved us as deeply and honestly as she did, my childhood wouldn't have been bearable. I knew we were "her babies," that usually she didn't even want to kill herself if we couldn't come too. I knew she was willing to do something Heavenly Father might not approve of (kill her children, to state it maybe too bluntly), and thus possibly sacrifice her own place in the Celestial Kingdom, just to give us the gift of a short life and an eternity of happiness.

I love her for that. And I love her much more for the fact that she never did it.

I love her more than words can say, and I also, sometimes, hate her- for not realizing that heaven isn't a place on a map.

And for the nightmares. Drowning, trapped in a car, my baby siblings tied into their car seats. I can't get them out, they're terrified, Mom's hair flowing in the water, hands off the wheel, letting us go. We can't breathe and she's letting us go. She's letting go.

NON-FICTION

Only Love Taps

By Nicole Melchionda

When I was thirteen, my brother tried to dismember his arm with a kitchen knife. I came home from school to an unusually empty house and found said weapon lying on the kitchen table. I later learned that he was escorted to a psychiatric hospital in an ambulance because he claimed he had a microchip implanted in him and that his family wasn't *really* his family. I didn't dare visit him once. While my parents left me alone in the vast four-bedroom home, I held that same knife to my wrist for a long time, fantasizing about my suicide.

I couldn't cut. I've never cut myself beyond the use of thumbtacks, a method my friend taught me when I was twelve because the marks usually faded by the next day and it rarely drew blood. The turning inside-out of flesh was still enough to feel punished. My brother spent years molding me into his self-loathing, anti-human, but, no matter how hard he pushed me to kill myself, I couldn't give in to what I believed was our desires. Somebody would have to find the body, and that fact alone is what kept me alive.

Ryan was a good kid. He was my best friend during my early years, and at the bottom of some box among many others in the attic are photos of us that represent my struggle to box my own depression: the feigned smile on Christmas Eve when, right after we took the family photo, I quarantined myself to my room and wrote in my journal that I wanted to die, the pages still stained with tears where the ink smudged; the photo of Ryan donning a smile and a thumbs up in his leg cast after my other brother, a pacifist, broke it when he snuck into his room while everyone else was asleep in an attempt to steal his belongings for pot money again; the picture of me smiling sleepily at a swim meet when, the night before, Ryan shook me violently as I pretended to sleep until he dragged me out of bed, my body thudding against the hardwood floor, and he beat me because I didn't wake up to tell him the password to log in to the computer.

I developed an alter-ego. No one really knew who I was. My mother only formally met me once she forced me to the doctor one day after she was finally fed up with my excessive absences from school. I begged her not to take me, that I wouldn't miss any more school, but she was afraid of what held her only daughter hostage, the baby she tried so hard to conceive after three boys. I didn't want to face a man who had all the power in the world to diagnose me and force my illness into the open where I could become even more ostracized. I already knew what I was harboring inside me. I didn't want some white coat pitying me.

Why are you here to see me today?

I am depressed. My mother's face tightened as she sat across the claustrophobic room, arms folded. I felt myself leaving my body.

What are your symptoms?

I can't get out of bed, I have no appetite, I am no longer interested in things that used to interest me, I am sad, and when I'm not sad I feel nothing at all. I provided the laundry list of symptoms I researched on Google before the appointment to make sure there would be no confusion or any reason to bring me back to the doctor ever again.

Have you felt suicidal?

All the time.

No, never.

I was not going to be strapped to a hospital bed on suicide watch.

I performed my duties as a circus monkey and was rewarded with a fast diagnosis. A two-minute conversation was enough to determine that I was mentally unfit to take care of myself. He suggested a therapist and the possibility of medication, but I refused both when my mother asked me later. To this day I've refused to see a therapist, partially out of pride, and I've never put anything in my body that could fuck me up more. I don't know if I inherited the depression from somewhere in my genes, but I always attributed my stubbornness to my father.

When I just started getting depressed, I took advantage of my mother's trust and lied that I was sick. Once I'd missed around a week of school, she suspected I just didn't want to do my work. I shoved fingers down my throat and showed her my vomit just to avoid any human interaction, because when I wasn't alone, I was no longer myself. To this day, I still carry on with my ritualistic smile and I show enthusiasm for everything just because I realized how tiring it is to answer the same questions every day about whether or not I was okay. Most people's first impression of me is that I'm ditzy, but that was okay with me because that judgement usually deterred them from really getting to know me.

It's not that I didn't want to talk to anyone, it's that no one could fix me. Their knowledge of my dark parasite only created more obstacles I had to hurdle when I could barely get out of bed each day. Only as I write this essay do I realize how painfully honest the lies to my mother really were, and my absences were, perhaps, necessary. Unfortunately, illnesses of the mind are not treated with the same devout attention as illnesses of the body.

"Depression is a dirty word," I wrote as part of my undergraduate senior thesis. I reticently chose the topic of studying how depression infiltrates a writer's work to not only learn about myself, but to attempt to de-stigmatize something beyond our control in this medical time period. I expected my teacher to force me to change my topic like many others had in the past, but she hungrily ingested each word and thanked me for opening her mind to empathy. She admitted to me during a conversation in her office that she had a schizophrenic nephew, and that my research helped her understand that we don't choose to be ill. After a decade of existing with my diagnosis, I was just beginning to find my voice and the confidence necessary to back up any assertions I made about this type of human experience.

My biggest regret and the most shameful moment of my life was telling Ryan I wished that he would kill himself so our family could get better and heal. It was true, his drug-induced states wreaked havoc on our once close-knit family. I only talk to my two other brothers on the phone once a year at most and see them every few years. My dad calls Ryan "The Hurricane." Despite how shambled my family is now, I'm ashamed that I could ever be cruel enough to tell another human being to die by their own hand. In that moment, I became my brother, and he became me.

93

"I've already tried three times," he said as he burst into tears, something he'd never done before.

I cried, too, which was an all-too-common occurrence for me at that time, and I held him tightly so he'd be bound to the earth. I hated him and loved him and wished he was never born and wanted to save him all while hating myself, too. My arms clung to him with rage and adoration as we sobbed about how irreversibly fucked up our lives would be so long as we each lived.

I was too young to understand when Ryan was Ryan and when he was high on all kinds of drugs. He abused me for around ten years of my childhood and adolescent years and, when he was high, he didn't remember what he did to me. One night, while I was sitting on the couch and my parents had gone to bed, he sauntered into the room and plopped down next to me with an almost empty bottle of wine in hand. He drank that whole bottle but was barely even buzzed. Even though I was the sober one, I can only recall fragments of the conversation that ensued. I told him that his assaults left bruises on my body.

His glazed eyes spilled alcoholic tears, perhaps pure vodka, and the haunting blue shadows the television cast upon his face made him look cadaverous. "I never meant to hurt you. Those were only love taps."

Healthy-minded people can easily make those who are depressed feel even more isolated. The reason why it took me ten years to finally own my disease is because of myriad rejections I faced in the past. In my freshman year of high school, one day I cautiously sat down someone whom I thought was my best friend. I'd known her since pre-school, she was the first friend I ever made, and we grew up like sisters. I managed to gurgle out that I had depression. She cocked her head in polite consideration for a brief moment, beamed radiantly, and chirped, "Just go on medication." She immediately got up and left me sitting alone. That was all she ever had to say to me about that subject, like most other things those days.

I tried vaporizing the sickness every way I knew how. I kept busy, I took up many hobbies, I ate well, and I exercised rigorously. When I was twelve, I almost instantly morphed from the chubby kid who ate her feelings into a svelte, curvaceous woman who received

94

compliments on her six-pack whenever friends snuck peaks during awkward changing room encounters. I swam six days a week for three hours each day, never missing a practice, selfishly showing up with plagues of flus, colds, and other highly transmittable illnesses. I became obsessed and, with a year's work, I went from being in horrible shape to the number one backstroker in New Hampshire and an invitee to swim at meets held at Harvard and in Europe. I used swimming as a scapegoat from my brother, and all the times I wanted to throw up from overexertion kept me from thinking about the physical, verbal, and mental abuse that was awaiting my return.

It comes as no surprise that I burned out. I slowly tapered off my swimming career and gained forty pounds in the year after I stopped. My brother told me I was fat, worthless, and unlovable, so that's what I became. In an attempt to gain control of my life again, I developed an eating disorder. Sometimes I would "fast" for days, sometimes I would binge, sometimes I would violate my throat with my hands until the bile came up. Some days I wouldn't leave bed, some days I would not allow myself to eat or do anything pleasurable until I ran ten miles. I maintained this lifestyle from when I was thirteen to seventeen before I left for college and knew I'd be living with others close by. I would no longer have the luxury to hide behind locked doors while I did my dirty deeds. I was sick of being sick, tired of being tired, and fed up with being fat. I started treating myself with kindness and, sure enough, the weight began to drop off. I slowly realized that, if I genuinely took care of myself, I'd be happier and healthier, even if the depression will always tear at my gray matter.

I started writing in order to combat loneliness. In one poem I wrote back when I was twelve, and embarrassingly believed every poem needed to rhyme and each new line had to be capitalized, I explained my compulsion:
I write to express my sorrow
All the emotions left unsaid
I write because my paper listens
When no one else did

As simplistic as it may be, it still burns through my sternum. My brother and all the hardships that have manifested in my life as a nurturing of his hate-spawn inside me have created the most frustrating contradiction. I write to intimately dissect myself, but each time I approach my brother lyrically, I spew fecal matter. Poems become forced and cliché, and nothing I write ever begins to encapsulate the complex thoughts and emotions I have, so there's this huge, essential part of myself that's forcibly untapped because I'm surmounted by ambivalence. I do not exaggerate when I say I have attempted hundreds of failed poems deserted in their fetal state about a man who never asks how my life turned out when my parents pick up the phone.

My mother chastises me for severing all ties with him, and sometimes I think I hate her. *He's your brother. He's your family. My sister gave me a black eye once. It's what children do. You have to talk to him at some point. You have to learn how to forgive. I think you're making this into a bigger deal than it was. He didn't sexually abuse you, did he?* But what she doesn't understand is that I think I have forgiven him, even if he's left fossils in my skin and reptilian reflexes in my brain. I harbor no resentment toward my parents for what happened, because I know how he abused them as well, how many of my mother's tears were locked behind her bedroom door, how they did everything they could to to quell the unquellable. I've let go of my anger and, any time I face my body dysmorphia in the mirror, I ask myself whose voice I'm really hearing. Yet no decent person would shame someone for quitting cigarettes or alcohol, so I don't allow my mother's criticisms to guilt me into relapse just because my toxin happens to be genetic. I know her intentions come from the right place. All she wants is to have a Christmas where everyone in the family can handle being under the same roof.

Despite the occasional whirls of encumbering grief that strike me late at night when I try to sleep, I am okay now—really okay, and not the kind of okay when I want to be left alone. I have to accredit most of my solidity to my boyfriend, George, who has stayed with me for over two years while dealing with my insecurities, guilt, jealousy, panic attacks, and crippling anxiety. He holds my hand when we go to the grocery store, since going alone is a terrifying feat.

He cradles me like a child when my lungs compress and sputter for air as my heart palpitates and I believe I'm actually dying. George is the only person I've allowed myself to be vulnerable with, the only person who has known and loved and cared for my body, the only person who has made me feel accepted, worthy, human. He taught me how to view myself through his eyes and not Ryan's.

Habits become instinct, though, when they've had a decade to become practiced and learned. Around six months into the relationship, I mistook George for the smallest splice of a second for Ryan. He raised his hand mid-stretch and I cringed. I thought he was going to beat it down into my skull. I feel like a changed woman, the woman I was supposed to be when I'm with George, but some things cannot be left behind. I tried my best to ameliorate Ryan's existence by composing the umpteenth failed poem about him, the last I believe I'll ever write uttering his name, "Ryan Anthony":

Ryan Anthony,
penultimate in the womb.
When I was three I thought we'd be
inseparable forever.

In the woods behind our house
I was the sorceress you feared.
But now I fear I'll not surpass
the strength those days displayed.

One night in bed my love raised
his hand. I registered it as yours.
Our amygdala whispered then
that he was going to kill me.

Ryan Anthony,
I wear your voice more
feebly each day, but mental
illnesses will never leave.

You may always have some grasp
no matter how long we've been estranged.

I'll still become the child crying
for lost Ryan Anthony.

      Though I get uneasy when I consider never talking to Ryan for the rest of my life, getting married without his attendance, having children with one less uncle, and having one less relative to hold when my parents die, I'm never going to sacrifice my growth for someone else who doesn't nurture my well-being, certainly never under the pretense that I'd be doing it for the sake of being a good anything—sister, friend, lover, etc. Perhaps he'd be surprised to know I still keep a collage of childhood photos with him hanging on my bedroom wall, but only the ones where I am no older than three: his warm embrace coming from behind my infantile body and my chubby fingers trying to reciprocate, but stabbing him in the eye as he endures it with a smile for the camera; Ryan excitedly grabbing his wiener on the maroon carpet of our first home as we sit across from each other, my arm reaching out for him in wonder, my mouth open in baby babble; a classic bathtub photo, where Ryan once again cradles his wiener, mouth comically agape and eyes rolled backward, his bronze skin juxtaposed with my paper skin.

      When I look at that cute, chubby, mystified-by-everything baby, I feel sorry for all she doesn't know is coming, that the little boy with skinny legs next to her will obliterate everything she once thought was good about the world. When I see that naked, fragile flesh, I remember how easily transformed my body was when broken blood vessels oozed.

      With years of nurturing and patience, I've been able to distance myself so much from that little girl that it feels like she is not me, that I was born at eighteen. Sometimes I feel her loss as my own, but I have and always will treasure what she learned through her grief. Although we know we will always possess the strength to rip ourself to shreds, we've learned we're stronger when we don't.

Dis-Order

by Heather M. Browne

"This is Dr. Heather Browne, may I help you?"

The voice was crying over the phone, "I need help. I need help Dr. Browne, but I...I don't think I can pay much. Can you help?"

"What type of help do you need?"

"Have you ever lost anything?"

My brain went to humor….my keys, pennies, maybe even my mind.

"I'm sorry, lost anything?"

"Yes. Do you know loss, Dr. Browne?"

Oh this poor, poor woman. Yes, sadly I do know loss. I lost both of my grandparents, my Mom when I was 16, my Dad, and just 10 months ago, I lost my husband.

"Honey, who have you just lost?"

It is a strange thought, "just lost", even stranger, to "have just lost", to have had and now lost, to have had someone there, maybe for a really long time, waking up each day and seeing their face, holding their hand, smiling at their wonderful laugh, hoping for their love or maybe just a hug. And then one day, one minute, for some, who knows why reason, they are gone. And nothing makes sense. And you don't know who you are without them anymore or what this life is without them. It is like part of you has become detached or separated. You are no longer a part of them, and all you feel is each part of you aching, without them. Loss makes no sense. You are disjointed, from yourself and from life. Like you no longer need your arms, because there is no one left to hug and you certainly won't be hugging yourself, but you need a hug, desperately. You don't need your legs, because there is nowhere you can run away from this.

This, it is everywhere, in you, under you, over you, and all around you. It's kind of like drowning, kind of like being in this horrible pond or a poisonous womb. Maybe this is what Hell is, not fire, not brimstone, not little red horns, but this unbearably heavy overwhelming loss that swallows you up, but doesn't spit you out. No fish, no disciple, no person, not even God can take away the reality of what you are drowning within in this very moment. Loss is the lack of, the total absence of. Everywhere you look all you can see is the loss of the life of the one you loved. Next time you go, they won't be at the park playing ball, at the restaurant eating fries, in their bed snoring or cooing. You can't tell them about your raise or call when you just need to hear their voice and to hear "I love you" one more time. You see their absence, the nothingness, everywhere. Which is crazy, how can nothingness be everywhere? How can you be surrounded by nothing, and yet feel that nothing everywhere, in every pore, every hair, certainly every breath that you still breathe, taking in and letting out.

What if you held your breath right now? Do you have any of their exhalation still left within you? Can any of their carbon still be in your cells, can you hold your breath so all of them is not already gone? But no, you can't. No matter how hard you try, at some point you have to exhale. And when you do you lose even more than what you've already lost. Maybe one, two, three, more cells, more of their carbon footprint, gone. With each exhale you are further away from holding on to who they were and who you are. With each breath, you are becoming more not, them, everything is out of order, dis-ordered, like a stack of cards all messed up so numbers don't fall in any sequence, and nothing that you see suits. Nothing suits.

But your heart, oh your foolish heart, frustratingly, keeps on pumping, automatically. If it were up to you, it would wear itself out, like a wind up clock that has no more ticks. If it were up to you, your lungs would stop expanding. Or better, yet, like a balloon, they'd just pop. You know there won't be any more parties or celebrations, no delightful cascade of sucky candies, no streamers, no confetti, just a loud massive bang, like a gun, or the crash in a car accident, or maybe the shock of that dreaded word, cancer. Instead of confetti, instead of candy, you only have tears falling, tears that are streaming down. And streamers look like limp veins and arteries that no longer send your loved one any more blood. Yes, I know loss.

She sobbed into the phone that she couldn't pay but she was falling apart. Her name was Karen and she was petrified for her kids,

100

six and eight, petrified that she wouldn't be able to care for them. He had been gone four months. Gone four months, one week, three days, and she was wondering if she was crazy because she was still counting. I was ten months, three days and hmmm, just over five hours.. So who was crazy? She said she thought she had been doing okay, for a while. He was in the grave and the marker had been laid, and she watered the flowers left there each week. She went to sit with him on his grave every single week. I had only gone three times in ten months. She went weekly. No wonder she felt crazy. I didn't feel him at his grave. I only felt my hurt, my sadness and my overwhelming loss. I hated speaking to him in the ground. And I was glad the grass was hard and scratchy. It hurt my hands and my legs each time I touched it. And I liked that pain. Not even green, but a pale nothing, lifeless gray. Kind of like the color of his face when he had died, gray, the sky on a stormy day. Every day now was stormy.

I wanted him in the sea, or better yet, on the top of a mountain. He didn't belong here. He didn't belong in that hardened place. And she didn't feel like she belonged here now too. The bills kept piling up, the kids were constantly fighting, and she was so tired. With death, you are so tired. Even in sleep, you can't stay asleep long enough to really rest. And your eyes burn and there's never enough moisture to soothe them, no matter how many tears fall. Reality rushes back in that second you open up your eyes, again. Your eyes are eyes that still open.

My husband died with his open, beautiful blue and sparkling. He had wonderful eyes, huge that you didn't get lost in because they found you. He had these big warm eyes that when he smiled made you feel like everything was going to be okay. Smiling eyes, that kept you safe in. Nothing was safe now. He was smiling when he died, smiling at something beautiful. And it wasn't me. He was smiling at someone else bringing him pleasure. I wanted to close them. But I didn't. Instead I kissed each one; I kissed them with my lips. Lips that had last kissed his just an hour before his death, and now would never again. I was wishing I could see what he now could see, instead of me only seeing all the gray, and him.

My right eye started to twitch a few days after my husband died. All on its own it kept twitching open and close, a momentary tease, hide and go seek, a sick and cruel game of peek-a-boo. Even my eyes knew they didn't want this new view. It was too much to lose.

Karen was still sobbing, harder now. She said she was losing things, her keys, glasses, a credit card. She kept hunting and hunting and would get into a frenzy, trying to find everything that she had lost. She said yesterday was the worst. She had fallen asleep, maybe for an hour or two. And she awoke to the phone ringing and when she picked it up it was the school and they were wondering where she was and why she hadn't come to pick up the kids. And she asked,

"Whose kids?"

"Yours, Mrs. Long."

She didn't even remember their names. She didn't remember she had kids or where they went to school, or where they lived, or what day it was. All she knew is that she was angry that they had awoken her. It was the first time in months that she'd actually fallen asleep without trying, without cd's, or TV, and alcohol. She had quietly drifted away, just like her husband had. Just like mine had with aquamarine eyes. Peacefully, without any fight or struggle, just the way it is to be when something stops, nothing was falling apart, or coming undone, no broken bones or busted skin, nothing out of order or out of place. He just quietly stopped. And it was quiet. If the school hadn't called maybe everything would have stopped. Maybe she'd never have to open up her eyes, and maybe her heart would give up beating, and her eyes would give up seeing, and maybe her lungs would stop stealing more and more air, because each breath was bringing her further and further away, from everything she had already lost.

GUEST EDITOR BIOGRAPHIES

Susan Spalt not only served as dis*or*der, mental illness and its affects guest editor, but also has submitted since its conception four years ago. She also lives in Carrboro, North Carolina. She retired several years ago after a long career in School Health specializing in trying to get people of all ages to do things they did not really want to do. Susan has written and loved poetry for much of her life. Her poems reflect her belief that poetry is not only for esoteric journals— but is part of everyday life. Her poetry has appeared in some unexpected places. She rhymed the school district's lice policy, and one of her poems was set to music to celebrate Carrboro's 100th anniversary.

Her poems have also appeared in numerous anthologies, including Annapurna, 2015 and Disorder, 2014, Red Dashboard Press and in Pinesong, published by the NC Poetry Society. Susan is one of four poets in Carrboro Poetica, a collection of poems published by Old Mountain Press in 2012.

Susan is a charter member of the Carrboro Poets Council which organizes and manages Carrboro's West End Poetry Festival. She is married to Allen Spalt and has two grown children and one grandson. Her latest publication, poetry, *Longer If It's Raining* is available on Amazon.com.

Joshua Gray serves as our alternate guest editor, and was born in the mountains of rural Northern Virginia, outside Washington DC. He grew up in Alexandria VA, two miles from the nation's capital and spent most of his adult life in the suburbs of the city. He attended Warren Wilson College in the mountains of western North Carolina, where he also spent the first few years of married life. Always in love with the mountains, he spent two years in Kodaikanal, Tamil Nadu, India from 2012-2014. He now lives in the DC area with his wife and two sons.

He has been published in many journals, including *Poets and Artists, Mipoesias, Blind Man's Rainbow, Front Range Review, Iconoclast, Zouch Magazine, Z-composition, Annapurna Magazine*, and many others. His poetry has been nominated for Best of the Net as well as featured on *Verse Daily's Web Weekly* section. For two years he was the DC Poetry Examiner for Examiner.com where he wrote reviews of poetry collections by local poets as well as articles on the local poetry scene. He is active on Twitter, Facebook, StumbleUpon and many other social media sites. Joshua judges poetry contests and edits anthologies for Red Dashboard LLC, he has also consulted on website design with RedD CTO.

Joshua has published four books, three with RedD—*Mera Bherat, Principles of Belonging, Symposium* and written an adaptation for children of the *Beowulf* epic, originally published by qarrtsiluni.com and edited by guest editor Alex Cigale, is available *from Zouch Six Shilling Press*! He also edited Pots and Sticks, a collection of poems by Charles A Poole, published posthumously. His recent book, *Steel Cut Oats* was released by RedD, April, 2015.

Zavia Willis our newest junior poetry editor was born in Westchester, New York, she now lives in Richmond, VA with her mother and younger twin brothers and a zoo of animals featuring birds, cats, a dog, fish and a rabbit – the stuffed penguin from her best friend is her favorite at most times. She published two poems in the 2009 and 2011 editions of the *American Library of Poetry*; she dabbles in the dark arts of science fiction and song writing posting her stories on *Fictionpress* under the pseudonym of *Hellsgun.*

She is a sophomore at Bridgewater College in northern Virginia, working on her English Major along with two concentrations in Digital Media and Multi-Media Authoring; grad school is in the thought pondering process to continue on towards Library studies. A help from her fanatic for music and horror movies, which helps inspires her killing off character scenes, generates new story ideas and is a cooping for when the brain decides to take an unannounced break. She is also a Staff Writer in her school's newspaper *Veritas.*

Derrick Paulson, Senior Fiction Editor received his M.F.A. in Creative Writing from Minnesota State University Moorhead in 2011, and is currently pursuing his secondary teaching licensure in Communication Arts and Literature at St. Cloud State University. He currently teaches high school and college-level English in central Minnesota. His works of poetry and prose have appeared in print and online in *365 Tomorrows, Annapurna, Canary, DisingenuousTwaddle, Orion Headless, The Gander Press Review, The Red Weather Journal,* and elsewhere. Between grading essays and trying to fit super heroes into lesson plans, Derrick alternates between spending time with his two sons and wife and spending his allowance at local collectible card game shops. Derrick judges poetry contests and edits anthologies for RedD, and edits manuscripts for the Dime Novel submissions. His first book was published in November, 2016—*Hot Potato: Misadventure Aboard the Good Ship Praxidike* is available on Amazon.com.

Ian Austin is our newest junior fiction editor, and is a junior English major at Bridgewater College, VA. He has received three silver key awards and an honorable mention from the Scholastic Art and Writing Awards for short stories. In 2013, he was published in the Scholastic Art and Writing Awards compilation book, *Raw Feet.* Three of his horror short fictions have been published in *Dark Moon Digest* magazine.

COVER ARTIST BIOGRAPHY

<u>Michael Baca</u> has been Red Dashboard LLC Publishing's Art Director since 2007. His art has appeared on numerous book covers as well as our anthologies. He works out of his studio in Pueblo, CO, where he also teaches challenged students art.

He works with mixed media on canvas, as well as digital works of art.

Other Red Dashboard LLC Publishing Books

Poems For A Beautiful Woman
Waiting For A Kiss
The Complete Pasquale
135 Years of Love
by Pasquale

Mogollon Picnic
by Rodney Nelson

Night-Crawl
by M.V. Montgomery

Principles of Belonging
Mera Bharat
by Joshua Gray

Memories of When We Were Birds
by Ray Sharp

The Hunger of Freedom
by Shelby Stephenson

Spirit of the Buffalo
by Kevin Heaton

Strange FrenZies
Z-composition Magazine

Unbridled
Cowboy Poetry Press

www.reddashboard.com\

THE DIME NOVEL IS
MAKING A COMEBACK!

Originating in the late 19th-century and seeing its heyday in the 1940s and 1950s, particularly in genres such as the Western, the format became an important influence on the comic book, the radio drama, and on film and television. Today's "flash novel" is really a new take on an old idea: stories just shy of novelette length, with numbered chapters rather than asterisks, and which, like the movies, compress a narrative otherwise "novelistic" in scope into a short form suitable for a single reading or download.

~ The Desert Dime Novel Trilogy ~

Mark Twain In Outer Space
The Double Dare Devil
Trouble In Paradise Valley
by M.V. Montgomery

Dime Novel Series

Ghost Cow Trail
by Doc Hudson

Be a part of our Dime "Flash" Novel project. Submit your 3500-7500 word manuscript for Western, Meta-western, Gothic fiction, Horror, and Noir fiction today!

editor@reddashboard.com

OTHER DIME NOVEL SERIES

Ghost Cow Trail
By Doc Hudson

The Maiden-head Mask
By Bill Plank

Sunset "Gold" Canyon
Wild Fire on the Brazos
By J.W. Edwards

Mall of the Damned
By Tyson West

The Santa Fe Trilogy—
The New Plateau
Ridin' High
By Kathleen Glasburn

Creating Florinda (English)
CREANDO A FLORINDA (Spanish)
By Anita Haas

Radio Tales
By Matthew Kirshman

The Bottle Opener
By Laura Madeline Wiseman

www.reddashboard.com

RED DASHBOARD
LLC